christine moore

LENT WORDS

QUILLKEEPERS PRESS

ISBN: 979-8-9891531-4-5

Published by Quillkeepers Press, LLC
PO Box 10236
Casa Grande, AZ 85130

Dear Reader,

There are times in my life when I intentionally unplug from gadgets. During these periods of reduced device interaction, time opens for other noticing. These are hours, days, weeks, or months of more sincere awareness of the world. Now, don't get me wrong. I can easily enjoy an online rabbit hole or a sofa binge-watching session. Many have taken me to inspirational, informative, enlightening and fun places. But creating a space to pay better attention to my own life and how that life intersects with yours, dear reader, is beautiful and essential. Most of the poems in these pages come from a period in which I gave up social media. In the time I might have been touring feeds, I wrote. Thank you for reading the resulting work. I hope you lose sight of me in the poems, and even more, I hope you find a sight of yourself. This is the wonder of words— to simultaneously find and lose ourselves. I have loved the words that I've laid down on these pages. I believe they have loved me in return. Now they are yours.

Gratefully,

Christine

Table of Contents

For my parents who made for us a world of music and wild fields.

Morning Prayer

I am destination.
Dust rambling around my legs
Ocher, dry-as-dry-straw grass knee high surround. Though,
I am not that.
I am of the trail worn by black and white
Holsteins whose single file unison
makes way for us children — etching their choreography,
a traceable language of theirs alone.
I am an adjective within. Invested. Invincible. Invisible.
My heart rushes in memory. My once 10-year-old body's
unconsidered desires alive again.
So the grass lures the heifer.
So the grass lurks
the grasshopper, the centipede, the owlet moth.
Lured are the California Towhee,
the Red Winged Blackbird, the mind
sat at a table awaiting the meaning of contemplation.
Or, at least, some understanding of how to get there.

Peacemaker

"After all, you cannot hide in the desert; there is no room for lying or deceit there." — John Chryssavgis

Her desert is a landing between upstairs and down. Lava monster red carpet tacked wall to wall and an enormous window of twelve or more feet overwhelms the girl, her folded body desperately working to be

the shape of a bridge,

a bird,

a soft place to land,

a punchline,   an ease.

She sets about attempting to love him, to like him, to hold him and heal him to reveal him, or   if she is very courageous,   to reveal herself to him.

She says (though not aloud), *you don't need courage, if you are not afraid.*

This breakdown may turn out to be the breakup. That's a funny word, isn't it?

If up is the destination of an ending, who will catch her when she falls?

And what is the role of truth in peace making, anyway?
There's her truth and her truth and her truth.
There's his truth and his truth and his truth.

The mountains are true, and the sky is true, the way it feels when you laugh so hard you cry is true. Her place in nature, her love of the wind and her wish to be able to whistle are true.

There's the truth of the morning: patient, abundant.
The truth of afternoon full of words and shape shifting.   The truth of night which howls and kicks and swallows   the bed whole.

Her landing is more of a corner. She becomes an expert on making the turn in both directions at once but doing so means she never touches down.
Floating in neither peace nor truth, she closes her eyes and wonders if she could weep.

Rooted and Rootlessnes

Always the same.
Each time.
Arrive. Blood
drawn to prove well
enough for the poison.
Upstairs to the chairs.

Always the same
hopes.
Each time:
Hope for a window seat.
Hope Arturo is my nurse.
Hope I take a nap.
Hope the Benadryl is intravenous.
I hope
it takes all day
so that this is an escape
as much as a rescue.

Always the same.
Rooted to the chair.
Rooted to the chemo.
Rooted to the other patients.
Our collective veins a tributary
or a deeply connected system of underground
growth.
I would live. Others would die.

Some years out, I often feel my veins and their veins
our blood rooted in some alternate time and
space where everyone is safe
and no family has an empty seat at their table.

There Is No Need for First Place Today

Let's create an agenda
in which everyone wins:
1. Send invitations.
2. Seek input from each voice, the women and
    children, the vulnerable and sick, the poor and
    marginalized, the imprisoned and isolated, the
    men — those who have sat in power and
    those who have not — the leaves on the trees,
    the bees, the creatures of land and sea, sky and
    beneath the soil, the wind and rain, the sun
    and air.
3. Listen.
4. Really listen.
5. Recall that love is abundant, abundance is
    abundant, we are abundant.
Call the meeting to a close the very
moment that all are in this abundant place.

A Rush to the Present

It's a whirl and swing sound. A whirl and swing
sound in water. It's nearly meditative — the Bosch
dishwasher running with dishes from a weekend of
letting them pile up in the sink.
Then there's the Sunday morning Premier League
commentator, his British accent detectable but not his
actual words, drifting in from the lounge.
There's a clock ticking and my dog, who turns four
in two days, gently gnawing on a yak milk cheese
stick. He is content.
Outside the sky has just gone grey after a glorious
morning of bright blueness. The grass in our backyard
is visibly wet with the night's rain.
My coffee is slowly growing cold because rather than
sipping and cupping it in my two hands, as if a
precious thing in need of my love, the mug sits on the
table between my arms and before my laptop as I type
this poem about rushing directly into the present.
I do not need the future. I have *here*. My mother's
thermal pajama bottoms on, my socked feet cold on
the battered wood floor of my kitchen, my hair up in
a haphazard bun with the front fringe hanging
somewhat annoyingly across my left eyebrow.
This is enough. This is enough. This is enough.

Caught off Guard

Things I'm certain of:

Nothing.

Turns out, I am caught off guard by this life.
Who I am?
Was I? Will be?
Caught off guard.
Conviction of status, impulses, motivations, wants, needs.
Don't have 'em... Not a one.
But that moment, as I sat
before this woman I'd only just met
to discuss your future, where you might
go to school,
I was certain
of just how much I love you.
because I was utterly caught off guard by
my joy in seeing you enter the room, late, humble,
kind. In all your high school *I know this campus* glory.
                    And me,
a foreigner in this world you spend your days,
overwhelmed with the simple, enormous moment of
meeting
                    you again.

May I live a life of unguarded humility.
May my certitude be that I know
nothing in this life but love.

Lent Words

These words you use
are on borrow.
Son, daughter, lover
influencer, dahlia—
we've merely been
lent their use. We will
one day give them back
as our tongues turn
to dust and our
lips ash.

This land, where I write,
once was the place of
other words. Distinct
dialects more than the
teeth in my head,
your head and your
head combined. Vowels
and consonants perhaps better
suited for the sun
that burns down upon
us or the river, whose
path we've redirected.

The call to name
and speak requires more
than cruel gestures, accusations
or channel surfing. Respiration
becomes phonation and
the vibration of it all
breathes life into our lives.

I can say, *you are my music.*
I can say, *yes, that is an owl.*
I see it, too.
I can say, *when I stepped*
outside this morning,
the clouds called me
to give thanks
for our existence.

Will This Be the Way of My River?

From atop the mountain, it begins:
A slow, steady drip, drip, drip of melting icicles
carving the smallest of paths in the snowpack.
Listen. The icicles to the left and right,
those behind and before are melting.
The sun, with no ambition or hidden agenda, simply,
gently, kindly warms the ice. Drip, drip, drip.
My small way
joins your small way
and her small way
and this small way
becomes a way.
A path to a stream   a stream to a river
flowing forward. Our water
reflecting the light of the sun.
Dazzling sunlight dancing the full width and length
of the river. Which we all know
will come to meet the sea.

Roast Potato Weather

Between where they put you in the ground,
and the sky where I've been taught you'd go
is where I live.

There are days in which this space
has room for feasts and art -- or at the very least, ease.
There are days in which this space
asks that I split myself into two
again   and again   and again.

Paul went in November.
I realize only now that his death was
a dress rehearsal for you.

How did I not see you had the lights
and lines of a full-on run-through?
How did I miss the chance to practice
being stagehand?

In January, as we lay
in bed together,
you ask
what will happen at the very last moment?

as though you were inquiring what temperature
I roast my potatoes.
I reply, as if doubt was not our bedfellow too:

you'll see Paul as clearly as you are seeing me
you'll take his hand and go.
And how, I ask, how will you speak to me then?
You say, our language will be:

Love within love;
knowing as much as knowing is known;
being to the extent that being is being.

Weeks later, it is cold and wet and Sunday.
It is roast potato weather.
I scrub, peel and half again and again and again
until the pan is full and oven has reached 450 degrees.
I set the table while time works away
in its subtle and sacred way.

All the Stars in All the Galaxies

There is no complete darkness.

No complete darkness.

No complete dark.

No completeness without dark.

Within the darkest dark matter, there are particles of light.

There is no complete pain.

No complete pain.

No completeness without facing our pain.

Within the darkest, dark pain, there are particles of love.

Within love, there is a healing space for pain.

A healing space for pain.

Love has room enough to heal pain.

Within the loving most love, there are particles of pain.

Within the brightest bright light, there are
particles of darkness

Light into light into light

Love into love into love

Dark into dark into dark

Pain into pain into pain
Pain into light into dark into love

Infinite unity. It is our
destination, and it is love that lights the way.

Persimmon Tree

All the big blue buttons on this dress and I haven't
time to tie my shoes. We must rush out, several-
seeded in our motives. Tuesday 6:00 a.m., the sky is
nearly complete, and the birds seem globular against
the day. We are moving away. She is the one leaving.

Virginian dogwood laughing in the foreground. White
paper sugar-dusted along the interstate. Someone must
have spilt a book along the road and lost track of
collecting all the words caught too up in noticing the
season changing like a metal pail nailed to aluminum
siding or the thinness of gold latticed in her hair.

I suppose I mean to go with her more for worry than for
want; and worry's want is never so strong as want's will.
She says the town is so old the red–white–blue porch
flags flap purple in the aged wind.

Says the county jail is a castle, but the abandoned paper
mill is astringent save for the black of shattered panes.
Says she slept her way into her slanted house whose
kitchen table, placed near the window, now leans
needingly on the south wall.

Slept her way because the slant makes waking difficult. And I must admit, I feel asleep even thinking of her leaving.

Old town, untied shoes, dogwood, and 6:00 a.m. The sort of things that end up downstream.

Grace

It is spring.
The birds know it.
Their song is joyful, giddy
trilling through the air.
What must they be calling out?
Come play! Come stay! Come, Spring!
And the trees. Blown this way and that, branches
torn and scattered through winter. They look near
an end. All covered in shabby, peeling
bark and surrender. And yet,
they call out to spring, too.
Come! Come now! We have saved our
reserves for you. Have us. Have all of us. We will
have you. We will take you into our bosom.
I see it.
The very tips
of the branches
the smallest of tender
green buds, perfectly formed mini
hearts each birthing to the world,
the sunlight,
the changing
reality.

-- DIFFICULT TELLEGRAM --

He was,

        of man

           would light his cigarette w/
             a soldering torch,

        feather-dust his liver in
              pellets.

        And me

             rattling the upstairs' walls
               fists upon
               the floor

               tossing chairs

               toward the ceiling

telling him *be still.*

Art Class

We gave every student
a sheet of paper,
a pack of crayons
and 10 minutes.
Draw a picture of God, we said.
Some drew. Some wrote lists.
The wind and the way chimes ring.
A single dad hustling to make
a paycheck,
a casserole, his
daughter's game.
Grey and brown,
smooth pebbles at the bottom of a stream—
determining the flow.
The quiet moment when you hear only
our own breath.
A lady pregnant   her belly broad, her eyes closed
her mouth in an expansive smile, her almightiness
one of generosity.
A celestial poet, eagerly describing life
across the stars.
A child full of awe and expectations.
An old woman rocking in her chair.
The sound of the sea when the waves are very large, and
the sound of the sea when the waves are very small.

A heart.
The clatter of two friends catching up
Forgiveness. Compassion. Rest.
A needle and its thread.

4.4.41

Your birth meant everything
to me for other reasons
deeper
more selfish.
The way you
sang Annie, Ella, Linda, Nat, or Rosemary.
The way you made pizza,
enough to feed every teen
piled into your midnight kitchen.
The way you listened to each poem
I wrote.

> Later, when you were sick,
> I'd hear you say your birth
> date to nurses, doctors and schedulers.
> I saw the thrill it gave them—
> how the date rolled from your mouth
> or blinked on their screen.
> Later still, when you could no longer
> speak, and I spoke for you,
> The thrill was, in a way, mine.
> Another gift given
> —a joy over a birth in the face of death.

Pleasure not because you laughed

at their joke or complimented

their outfit

but just

because

you were born

on a day

that is

fun to

say.

4.4.41

Familiar Arrangement

Today was not unlike most days. I thought of you. I thought of writing to you. I opened your book. You cupped my ear then, and this air of yours filled me. This, of course, is improvised. My ritual. I'll begin again tomorrow. Your book whole on the table I put beneath it last evening. The etymology of imagination folded in the drapery.

Swallowing the pages, like I had before. Tearing the binding and licking where the words made themselves paragraphs. Phrases reduced to consonants. I chewed. The vowels of it all stained black across my fingers, like your glass of water placed beside the flowers.

I ran my hand through my hair, and the etymology of imagination fell around my shoulders.

Stay Amazed

It is important to feel *of.*
Of nature. Of life. Of this.
     Of.

A morning walk can help.

The seasons on show even
along suburban blocks.

Notice the day's sounds.
Find yourself *of* them.

The trill-trill-threep of
Black Phoebe. The bold

definitive cheep-churp of
House Finch, and

the call and response qwoo-qwoo of
the mated Mourning Doves

then, further along, joins
the clank-clink in a stream

of running water of a morning cereal bowl
being washed. This person,

in their home, with their window
ajar because it is summer and the

heat is coming later, is *of*
it all. Their *of-ness* as distinguishable

as bird song. Not the clatter-clonk
of a dinner plate nor the ting–ting

of flatware. This is the sound of
cleaning up after breakfast.

I wonder:
Is it their own bowl?

I wonder:
Why is the earth beautiful?

Why is the Earth Beautiful?

The earth is beautiful so that
sometimes, while doing dishes,
sunlight can stream in from the window
and turn the bubbles on the back of
your hand to a scattering of rainbows
resting on your flesh.

It's beautiful so that when you're
in a hospital room the churning
sound of the monitors
will remind you of the cicadas'
hum from your island holiday,
the ever-present vibration matched
only by your blood flow in its essential
reliability.

When your friend calls with news of her
divorce and mentions through tears that a
hummingbird has just passed by, you know
the value of the earth's beauty then.
It is to remind her that there is ease
awaiting her— even if just a fluttering.

Or when you take the time to look up
and find reason for pure awe at the
sky above you, the beauty of the earth
makes sense then too.

The earth is beautiful
because she loves you. And like a true
lover, she gives and cares and nurtures.
She feeds you sweet fruit and makes
a place for you to shelter.

It is her reassuring beauty
that calls me to jump into the lake
whose depth terrifies even
as I remind myself that this
is the closest I will come to flying
—my feet moving as if wings; my body
suspended 1,600 feet above ground.

You see, I don't have a concise
answer for Earth's
extraordinary beauty.
But I do believe she
gives artists
something to reach for

and poets something to
praise.

In her love we make
love and music and dance
and work and play.
She is beautiful. We must
stay amazed.

East 19th Avenue

I brought with me a moment
of their future. My past alive
in their present. We moved together:
wrapped in a long, narrow fabric—
a bright and sturdy ribbon joining us as one.
My festooning the kitchen
with warm fragrances and silky
sauce intertwined with
the laughing and chatter
that danced its way toward me.
Their fruits our faith.
Their sofa our settee.
It was all new.
It was all eternal.
Candles lit.
Table set.
We lay down
deep beneath
the rush of time
and dined.

A Lesson in Letters

"Poetry itself is a ceremony, a ritual that allows for resilience." —Jane Wong

There are words at my hands,
words at my feet.
They tumble down around me.
They creep up within me.
Outlast.
      Accept.
      Laugh.   Hope. Rest.   Metamorphosis.
I make my own
alphabet:
one that bares this weight;
one that navigates this deep
relentless
and blue ocean;
one to rest safely within.
My alphabet has as much space for
love as it does for work,
and you are there too.
Together, we make the words
we need
for what
we do not know.

Not a Transformation

Nature, be my mentor.

Show me how you turn sun and
CO_2 to structure and sweetness.
Teach me how you draw
from sea and softness to form mother
of impenetrable pearl.
How can your coral be
airport terminals? How do your infants
emerge from silken homes with wings?
Fire, we have said, is the greatest gift. And we have burnt
classrooms and coaches. But our bodies are
gentle. Our insides are the lightest of elements:
calcium and cobalt.
It is easy to imagine God
forming us of clay, isn't it? Reaching hands down
into the sludge and silt and emerging with handfuls of
life. Then, ever so lovingly, shaping a shape meant
for care and discovery, for question
asking and free will.
If only we could listen now
to the lessons of the ooze and slush of our making.
What stories would the swamps share?
How should we live here?
Please, tell us.

Awaken

One day, I thought

                   I saw my soul.

               It was pink and hoovering
just outside of my body.

I had been meditating and
I could feel my center most
self in vibration.

         The moment I recognized it was the
              moment it   disappeared.

              Smugness is a great flaw of mine.

One afternoon, I fell asleep
while nursing my youngest.

We were on the sofa, tv on
and my son, her brother,
was down for a nap in their shared room.

He must have woken up and come out
to find us asleep.　　　　　He did not wake us.

He joined us on the suede sectional and used the
remote control to put on Sesame Street.

His body

Just outside of mine.

Her body just outside of mine.

Our Bodies just outside of one another's body.

This is how it was when I woke.

Outcome Unknown

You are the one
who has saved me.
And I am the one
who is saved.
Your hands large
enough to hold it all.
All of it, including at this
moment, me.
Admission.
She was admitted.
What shall I admit?
My inability to see the
outcome?
My focus on the
income?
Where do need and greed
intersect?
I am not my brokenness.
Though, wouldn't it be wonderfully
convenient and comfortable if
I was?

Sisters, They Swim

I.

When we move
We make a single spiral
Arms stretch towards
China navels
Lips meet in shared breath

No waves
No buoy
And all the salt
Is ginger

II.

Divided   her name is mine

We never rise
To face the myth
That life will have
More for us than   this.

Eternal Life

Blue and slightly the shape of a dove in flight is the space I can see in the clouds. From here, it looks just large enough to hold all of eternity in it. Or the yellow smattering of buttercups in the backyard. Each of their individual buds, too, seem just large enough to hold all of eternity. As do the photos coming back from Webb, its hexagonal mirrors working in unison to capture not hundreds but countless galaxies. Galaxies. Countless numbers of galaxies. They, too, seem the right size to hold all of eternity. And here we sit, holding eternity within ourselves.

What Remains

When the density of love,
once the weight needed to
tether you to this place,
sits oppressively on your bones;
find me in the breath
of wind that lifts around you.

When words become unreachable,
and you yearn for a better language
—one that makes material the things lost,
know me in the clamoring of life.
I am the waves reaching shore.
I am the kettle's whistle.

When all the color of actual
importance drains from your vision
—the horizon itself no longer holding
a space for earth to meet sky,
do not close your eyes;
look more closely at one another.

I am there.

Insecurity Makes Certitude Attractive

Do you think that naming your emotions
would help you get along with them better?

Like, this is George, my anxiety. And Alice, my grief.
Here is Dale, and here is Nina. They're my anger.

What would you name yours?
And how would you introduce each to me?
Would you welcome them into your home?
Would you ask them along to the hospital?

Or maybe that's not how it works.

Perhaps they arrive places before we do. Waiting there
for us. George and Alice anticipating my arrival.

The fact of the matter is that I just don't know.
I can't see what tomorrow will bring, and that tight ball
of Dale in my stomach isn't helping me see
any better.

Breathe. We forget to do that often. As if we're saving the

oxygen for some other use. There are insecurities of every shape and size. Time insecurities, wealth insecurities, looks and personality, love and hope insecurities. Air, for now, at least, we have that in abundance. Use it. Use the luxurious glut of each breath.

Questions at the End of a Decade

Have you made good intentions and failed?
Have you visited Crete?
Have you dropped your youngest off at preschool and
cried in the parking lot?
Have you bought a new car?
Watched your son grow almost entirely into a man?
Have you wandered the sacred rocks of Sedona?
Climbed the Kachina Woman and been blessed?
Have you discovered a favorite taco shop?
Have you quit social media only to join social media?
Have you read a good book?
Seen great art?
Started therapy?
Gotten a dog and a tattoo?
Met a soulmate?
Have you bathed your mother and
buried your mother?
Switched to decaf? Taken up taiko?
Tried chemotherapy, fentanyl and frozen yogurt?
Have you lifted your hands off the handlebars
and cruised – even for just a moment?
Pinned a boutonniere on your son,
survived a pandemic, fought with your siblings?
Have you questioned your faith and mourned
the death of countless strangers?

Have you had a good night's sleep?

Drunk too much wine?

Have you happily discovered your daughter to be better at most things than you?

Have you been held by a man who loves you?

And have you held him back?

Have you sat with a friend on the darkest of days?

Have you laughed?

Have you regretted the past and feared the future?

Have you coaxed a butterfly to land on your hand?

Have you stayed in touch?

Published a recipe? Perfected a lesson plan?

Have you made yourself ready for *this*?

Planting Season

We are together.
Though, in truth,
I am on my knees, she
is stood above me
so that, momentarily, she
appears taller.
Her hands are my hands.
Her hands are my mother's hands.
Beautiful hands:
slender,
      long,
            capable.
I can see that our hands
are beautiful hands
when I watch her use them.
We set about moving
hands in different ways.
I push holes into the soft,
blacker than black soil --
my fingers quickly caked
and powdered.
She nimbly opens each
paper envelope: *Careful.*
Careful. Try not to spill.

She tilts an envelope
into her palm.
We look together at what
scatters out.
The smallest seeds
just only slightly
larger than dust.
The larger ones are recognizable
for what they'll produce.
This white oval will be
cucumber.
Each seed (every one)
is clearly discernable
in its status as a beginning:
small,

      misshapen,

           dense,

                vulnerable,

           mysterious,

      whole.
She places a seed or two
into each awaiting opening.
Then, together, we
cover over the seeds

with soil, and water
the ground.
Our waiting becomes
a joint effort, too.
We watch in the evening
from our kitchen window.
We watch from our kitchen
window each evening—
eyes focused,
looking out at what
we hope we have begun.

Half-Headed Boys

Born the beginning-end
of some maroon
day,

      we are
a leap year;
a longitudinal bomb;
a language gaining words and speed.

      We run
      shoeless
through beet fields
—   the frozen roots
bleeding upon our flesh.

      We snap
      pencils
with our forefingers,
jump from
thatched roofs,

and eat onions

in bites the size of crabapples.

Our clouds are

silver soldiers

stapled to the sky.

Woodcut eyes

are made and lost,

after all, we're in

our father's land.

Acknowledgments

I wish to thank Terry, Rowan, and Annabel for being my most steadfast and trustworthy audience. Were it not for our dinner table talks, much of this work wouldn't exist. I also wish to thank Stephanie Lamb for her thoughtful feedback and creative attention to the poems. I am grateful to work with Quillkeepers Press.

About the Author

Christine Moore grew up in rural Northern California surrounded by nature. Her childhood was spent in large part outdoors, where she learned the joy and fragility of life. She holds an MFA in poetry from the University of San Francisco. Her work has appeared or is forthcoming in *The Pasadena Review*, *Interim*, *26: C A Journal of Poetry and Poetics*, and *Pinhole Poetry*. She is a mom, a wife, a food and wine columnist, a creative writing instructor, a cancer survivor, A California Poet in the Schools, and facilitator of a women's group in her community.